I LOVE ME!
JOURNEY TO SELF-LOVE

Copyright © 2019 Rebekah L. Pierce
All rights reserved.

No part of this book may be used or reproduced in any manner whatsoever without the express permission of the author and publisher. Brief quotations, with attributions to the book's title, may be used.

Published by The Pierce Agency LLC/RLP Productions
www.thepierceagencyllc.com
www.rlpproductions.com
804.549.2884

Rebekah Pierce Back Cover Photo Courtesy of Latika Lee

Cover Design by Sassi Concepts

Printed in the U.S.A.
ISBN-9781093424584

For reprint permission, or to use text or graphics from this publication, e-mail your request to rebekah@thepierceagencyllc.com.

I LOVE ME MORE:
A JOURNEY TO SELF-LOVE

By:
Rebekah L. Pierce, AA, BA, MA

Dedication

I dedicate this book first and foremost to the Holy Spirit, Jesus Christ, who has walked with me and sometimes carried me through every step of my life. I am fully aware that His hand is on me.

To my mother, Genovia Oglesby, who has always been the example for the power of faith in God, and who has supported me in almost everything I have decided to do in my life. I LOVE this woman.

To my siblings, Ann, Jeff and Michael, you guys are the best blessing to my life. How many people have siblings who back them up no matter what?!

And to my children, Immanuel and Macy, I'd do it all over again just to have the two of you. You are the LOVES of my life! To Eric, I've always loved you and always will. Thank you for loving me as I am.

To all of my supporters and fans, thank you so much for riding on this journey with me. I pray this book blesses each one of you.

Introduction

Many years ago, I heard a motivational speaker talk about the cards one is given when they are born. He said that regardless of the cards we are given - social class, health, education, family, etc. - those cards did not define us nor did they tell our entire story. That, it's what we do with the cards we are dealt that ultimately creates who we become.

There are many of us who feel that we have been dealt a very ugly hand. Struggle and pain seem to follow us wherever we go like a stalker. We wish we could swap cards with someone, anyone, in fact, who appears to have a much better hand. For example, one of my favorite shows used to be "American Idol." I loved the show because it presented people chasing their dreams like me. But then it also showed something much bigger and uglier: people chasing *other* people's dreams. You could tell who these people were because they bragged about how good they were and how everyone loved to hear them sing. Then, the inevitable happened. They got in front of the judges and were told no, emphatically. The camera would follow them out of the room and into the lobby or streets panning in close as the rejected "singer" cussed vehemently at the camera. Their equally angrier families followed the "singer" in dismay and shock that their child was not moving on to the next round.

These people were chasing other people's dreams. They didn't like the cards they'd been dealt and instead of making the most out of them, they convinced themselves that someone else's cards were worth getting. Well, that is just a waste of precious time and energy. We are only given one life to live. We should live it to the best of our abilities using the gifts that were given to us to make it an exceptional life.

And this is the goal for my life and the goal of this book: to encourage you to live a purpose-driven life guided by love. To discover a way to make the best out of the cards you were dealt in the hopes that you will learn along the way to love who you are and thrive on the gifts that were given to you when you came to earth. The stories that I share here in this book are designed to show you how imperative it is that you learn to love who you are so that you can receive the blessings that are waiting for you. We were not brought here to suffer and be in pain, but many of us are doing just this not necessarily because of a physical ailment, but rather a mental one. Our negative thoughts are ruling are lives; we are stuck in our past where bad things happened to us and we don't know how to let go of it and live in the present moment. That's also what this book is about: how to live in the present moment. How to change your thinking to change your life.

How to Read This Book

I Love Me More is not your typical "how to" book or memoir. This is an "I Am..." book. Each chapter begins with a glimpse into some of the experiences that shaped my thinking about who I thought I was before I made the decision to reclaim my life and my joy at the end of 2017. Within each chapter is also a post and its corresponding image that I shared on social media throughout 2018/19 when I started my journey to self-love. Finally, at the end of the chapter is a homework assignment (I can't help but to always be in teacher mode 😊) designed to spark a moment of clarity and understanding for your life. I encourage you to try these assignments. I also want to encourage you to share with me your thoughts via email or on my social media pages.

So, let's begin with the post I shared on my Facebook page about "American Idol." I have big dreams for my life: always have. In fact, this book is a major part of my dream. It is my fervent prayer that this book will open up the doors to speaking opportunities for me so that I can continue to encourage women and girls to reclaim their authentic voices and purpose. In short, I am working in my gift as a writer and speaker, but what happens when we do not like the gift(s) we have been given because it's not "sexy," and we start chasing other people's dreams?

Post from 2/6/19

One of my favorite shows was "American Idol," and I loved that show because it showed people chasing their dreams - like me. But then it also showed the great folly in chasing someone else's dream. Life is too short and too precious to waste energy chasing what is NOT for you. Don't put boundaries on what the Divine has for you because you want to be "like Mike." If only you'd love yourself enough to see that YOUR gift and the blessings that'll come when you "live" it is far grander and greater than any title that the world could ever give you. ♡ #wellnesswednesday #ILoveMeMore www.rebekahlpierce.com

Homework

What is your dream? How do you know that it belongs to you? List 5 things/events that confirm and affirm that "this" is what you were born to do.

Prologue

My Cards

My father left our family when I was 12 years old. It was Christmas Day and I remember after opening our gifts, he exited my parent's bedroom with a suitcase and simply walked out and never came back. He got into his car and drove away. I remember the big, beautiful Christmas tree sitting in the middle of our living room; it was surrounded by tons of gifts reflective, of course, of the four children he had fathered and up to that point, had been helping to raise.

I often say that when my father left us that day, he took his money and education with him. My mother was a high school graduate who had dreams of going back to school for nursing, but he had always managed to squash her dreams with complaints of there not being enough money for her to do that. Yet, he managed to get three degrees. My mother had to account for every dime spent or asked for. I remember asking him for a quarter once and he proceeded to lecture me on how hard it was to earn money. I was about eight years old. He did not give me that quarter.

He also kept my mother away from her family whom she was close to. Both of my parents had grown up in Pleasantville, NJ and married right out of high school. He then joined the military which required them to leave NJ. My dad served in the latter half of the Vietnam War right before I was born in 1972. They were stationed in Missouri where all four of us were born (my sister and I at Whiteman Air Force Base), and when he got out of the service, he started chasing the money; he had earned a degree in Engineering and took jobs in Massachusetts, Missouri, Illinois and then finally, Stockton, California. The further away he could keep my mother from her family, the better. When my grandmother died, my mom was 32 years old and had not seen her mother in years. She was devastated!

But we lived in nice homes on the "right" sides of town. My mother loved home interior decorating, so although he never really wanted to give her money to buy anything for herself, she was able to take what money he did give and decorate our homes. And they were beautiful! We did not go without food or clothes because my mom used what her mother had taught her: sewing skills, cooking and baking from scratch and cleanliness. I learned how to do all of these things from my mother.

I saw my father hit my mother once; he had returned to the house after leaving that Christmas Day to get a few more of his things, I guess. He and my mother were talking in the living room, or arguing, because the next thing I saw was my dad strike my mother with an open fist. Then, I saw her reach for a candelabra sitting on the table by the door and throw it at him. He had escaped through the front door just in time; it hit the wall instead of him. That memory stuck with me for years; it followed me into adulthood and into my relationships as a young adult.

My father left my mother for another woman, but not just any woman. He left her for a white woman with money and a big house. She had what my mother did not. This would become a modus operandi for my dad: he'd take the woman for everything she had and then leave her for another woman with more or better. He'd destroy not only those women and their children in the process, but his relationship with us as well. In the few times I saw him during my teenage years, he wasted no time in telling me that I was never going to be anything. That I was like my mother: poor, black, nothing. I argued vehemently back that I was going to be somebody, but he had planted a seed when he threw those words at me. Those seeds would grow into a harvest of self-doubt and low self-esteem.

We'd spend the next six plus years of our lives in Stockton living in run down houses that should have been condemned, in homeless shelters, or temporary stays with family and friends. We went hungry often and had to go to work with our mother at nursing homes (she was a CNA); the smell of aging and death haunted those buildings. I hated those places. There were no new clothes for the beginning of school, no lunch money. We went from attending schools on the "best" side of town to the "hood." Drugs and gun raids by the police were a common thing at my high school in the mid-80s. Then there were the gangs. Both of my younger brothers joined the Crips, so being shot at or avoiding certain people or neighborhoods because your brothers were in a rival gang from the one that dominated a certain part of town was nerve-wracking.

I was an angry, sad, lonely, abandoned teenage girl. I was knock-kneed with crooked teeth. I wore coke-bottle glasses, big, baggy clothes to hide my body and kept my nose buried in a book. Reading was my escape. I could disappear from hunger, fear of being shot or my brothers being killed and the understanding that my mother was in survival mode. She worked 3-4 jobs to help take care of us. My dad had disappeared again - angry perhaps because a judge had refused to give him custody of my brothers and break us apart (I'd learn later on that he wanted my brothers to claim them on his taxes.). There was no need. My mother was a good mother who did what she could to take care of us.

My self-worth and self-esteem were in the toilet. I just knew that no one loved me or could. I had nothing to offer, I felt. But I had two things going for me that I'd come to learn to lean on because my life depended on it ... literally. First, my father did leave one great thing behind him when he left. The Lord. You see, we grew up in the Pentecostal church. My father was a pastor at one point; he pastored a church which made my mother the first lady. My parents loved the Lord. I remember hearing songs by Andrae Crouch and James Cleveland being played constantly on the record player in our home. Those gospel artists and many others were played on the stereo in our home constantly. My favorite song was "Amazing Grace."

We had learned about the Lord early in our lives. The Father, the Spirit and the Holy Ghost was the way to Christ: The Trinity. So, I knew as a young child about the gospel. I knew who had made me. I knew who I belonged to. We were all baptized as children. But when my dad left the church, we did as well. However, my mother never left God and so we continued to know Him through my mother's prayers and steadfast devotion to His Word. I am a living testimony that there is nothing more powerful than the fervent prayers of a mother.

The second thing I had going for me was school. I loved to read as I've previously mentioned. My first books were given to me by my mother: the *Strawberry Shortcake* series. I would bury my nose in those books and more like *The Hardy Boys* and *Nancy Drew Mysteries*, anything by Agatha Christie, the Harlequin Romances and Louis Lamar westerns. Soon enough, I was inspired to write my own stories. And my mother encouraged this (and still does).

Before my father left, I was an average student, but when he left, I needed a distraction from the pain of abandonment and fear because many things were uncertain in our lives at that time. So, I got lost in school. From junior high school well until graduate school, I was an Honor Roll student. I had to be. My identity became wrapped up in learning - in writing and reading. My teachers in high school (Mrs. Pratt, Mrs. Davenport and Coach Wang) encouraged me to learn and to develop my gift for writing. I remember when my guidance counselor, Mr. Steele, a balding old white man, told me that I could not go to college because I was not smart enough. I had a 3.84 grade point average.

What he meant was that I was a *black girl*, and education was not for me or anyone like me. When I told Mrs. Pratt (my English teacher), Mrs. Davenport (my History teacher) and Coach Wang (my track coach), they were LIVID. They each told me not to listen to Mr. Steele, and they each wrote letters of recommendations to the colleges of my choice (I was accepted into all of them). Coach Wang is the reason I was the only Airmen in my basic training flight to be chosen to pick the career of my choice (health care) because he wrote me a letter of recommendation for my recruiter. Can you imagine how many kids' dreams my guidance counselor destroyed with his beliefs about people of color? I was blessed to have people who believed in me.

But even though I excelled in school, I still struggled with loving and liking myself. I knew that I had something special inside of me, but it was trapped behind self-doubt and loathing. I hated to look at myself in the mirror because I didn't like what I saw. I thought I was ugly and worthless. I never smiled and soon developed a reputation for being mean. My nickname was "Evil Lynn," and boy, did I carry that name well, but it wasn't accurate. I had a few friends who saw the real me - funny, loyal, but serious. I would fight anyone for my friends. I'd even fight a boy if I heard he was telling false stories about me or them. Shout out to Arthur and Vincent for pulling me off of that boy's neck that lied about having sex with me when I was a virgin. 😊

I was also teased about how I spoke - "like a white girl." And my name was REBEKAH, which I never let anyone call me. Remember also that I went to the best schools on the "best" side of town where I was the only black girl most of them time before our father left. When I had to attend a middle school and high school "in the hood," I was a target because I was not like other black girls. I spoke proper English and carried myself in a different manner. I went to class every day and studied hard and I played sports: I ran the hurdles and was the goalie for the soccer team. But even more importantly, I had big dreams. I wanted to be an English teacher and a writer. I also wanted to get out of Stockton, California alive. I knew instinctively that being "different" was going to be my ticket out of town.

And my mother encouraged each of us to not only have a dream for our lives, but to follow them. However, I still wasn't much different from many of the black girls (girls in general) at Edison High School. I was fatherless, angry and poor. And when I got mad, every cuss word in the world came spewing out of my mouth. It was wrong, but I was just so angry and stressed. Needless to say, no matter how much I hated that nickname, "Evil Lynn" stuck.

By the time I was 18, my whole world was education. My mother had told my sister and I repeatedly to get our education first and a man second because if he left, we'd have something to fall back on. She did not, and that is why she wanted her daughters to be better prepared. Now, this does not mean that my mother believed that her daughters were going to automatically be divorced one day. My mother was hurt; she'd been rejected and denied the opportunity to achieve her dreams. She was spending every waking moment of her life trying to take care of four children working as a CNA.

It was hard for her, especially with no family nearby to help her. Her mother had died a few days before I turned 12, and as I mentioned earlier, she had rarely seen her mother since leaving home at 18 years old. Watching my mother in this struggle was enough of a motivation for me to get my education and make a better life for myself. I was going to be an English teacher and a writer come hell or high water. I was going to get my Ph.D. in Literature and write the great American novel. Big dreams, right?

Then I tried to kill myself. The college I had planned to attend sent me a letter rescinding its offer because I had failed Algebra II. They wanted me to go to summer school and earn a C or better, otherwise, I could not go. I was devastated! I read the letter as saying I was stupid and was never going to get out of Stockton, California. I was destined to be nothing just like my father had said. The only way out was to die, I thought. So, I swallowed a handful of pills (I didn't even know what they were) that I'd found in my mother's room.

As I laid down on my bed with the last few pills from the bottle in my hand, crying so deeply, I began to think about what my death was going to do to my mother. All that she had been through and now I was going to put her through this. *This can't be the way it ends.* I heard the Lord say, "This is not your story," and then I remembered a dream I had when I was five years old. A light had come and wrapped itself around me. I felt safe and loved in that light. It shone so bright on me and I could feel His presence. I remember looking up and seeing His face as only a child could imagine. I knew I was loved.

That memory came back to me that day in my bedroom. He was there in that room reminding me that I was His and that I was going to have another story. I put those pills in my hand back into the bottle and went to sleep. It was time to create a new story for my life with the deck of cards I'd been dealt, but it was going to be a long journey filled with many bumps in the road and plenty of ghosts around the corner.

> DECIDE WHAT KIND OF LIFE YOU REALLY WANT... AND THEN, SAY NO TO EVERYTHING THAT ISN'T THAT

Post from 1/28/2019

The "decision" is (and always has been) up to you. I want to encourage you on this #sassysaturday to "decide" to say no to everything (and anyone) that doesn't add joy, love, value and abundance to the life you are building. Let's "decide" to build (create) our "life" today. ♡ #ILoveMeMore

www.rebekahlpierce.com

Homework

What are two (2) things you can do today to "create" the life you want?

I LOVE ME MORE!!

Chapter 1 ~ I Sent My Representative

"Be soft. Do not let the world make you hard. Do not let pain make you hate. Do not let the bitterness steal your sweetness" (Unknown).

I first fell in love with a young man when I was 17. Oh, how I loved him! I shared with him my dreams and encouraged him to chase his as well. He loved me for who I was, a knock-kneed girl who wore coke-bottle glasses with wild hair and dreams bigger and wider than the Pacific Ocean. He was my first EVERYTHING. And then he broke up with me for a girl who had what I did not: material things, her own place and access to weed. So much for love. I was rocked to my core ... again. I had been rejected and abandoned ... *again*. Like my mother, I didn't have anything of material substance to offer him. I thought that I had told him too much, was too outspoken in my beliefs. I just wasn't good enough for him or for anyone, I felt.

At first, I thought about getting pregnant on purpose to keep him. I honestly thought that because that's what many of the girls/women I knew directly or indirectly were doing. But then I thought about my dreams of being a teacher and writer, and I knew I could not/would not give them up for any man. I had seen what happened when a woman did that. I remembered what my mother had said to me: "If he really loves you, he'll come back to you." I'm sure you can guess my response to that: *Yeah, right*! And so, I closed myself off. I didn't want to feel that kind of pain ever again. I vowed to never let anyone get that close to me.

    I soon left Stockton for college. I had achieved one of my goals. I was more than eight hours away from home and on my own. I was lonely, but proud of myself. I was the first of my siblings to go to college. My mother was so proud (my father was *completely* absent from my life at this point). And then I met *him*. I was a sophomore in college at UC Santa Barbara and he was a Marine.

    I met him on a trip to Tajuana, Mexico with my sister who was a student at San Diego State University by then. I thought he was so tough and masculine. He wasn't afraid to speak his mind about things and he was protective. He had big dreams, too, and I soon found myself opening up to him. I let my guard down. Big mistake. It started with name-calling: "you're stupid, you're fucking retarded." Then he started grabbing me so hard, he put bruises on my arms. I used to say that I would never get caught up in an abusive relationship because my mouth was too big, and I was too strong-minded. Wrong again!

This man broke me down emotionally. And then to cement his control over me, he raped me on the bathroom floor of my apartment while my roommates partied in the living room with some friends. I never drank alcohol before college. I saw what it did to people, and I didn't like the idea of losing control of myself, so I refused to indulge and caught hell for that from friends. By the time I was a sophomore in college, I had drunk alcohol at least once and had found that I had an extremely low tolerance for it.

At the party that night, I let him bully me into drinking. I don't recall what I drank, but I do recall not feeling well. I do recall the room spinning. And I do recall saying "No" when he took me into the bathroom and proceeded to push me down onto the floor.

I'd never felt physical (and emotional) pain like that, and I remember lying there crying. I had been violated, but because he was my "boyfriend", I knew there was no point in telling anyone what had happened. I kept silent … about the rape (and would do so until a few years ago). I did, however, tell my mother and sister about the abuse and they encouraged me to break up with him.

I did that ... sort of. I had decided to join the military that year because tuition was being raised my junior year and I knew I wasn't going to be able to afford it. I was already in a lot of debt with my student loans and my mother did not have any money to help me. So, I joined the Air Force at the encouragement of my "boyfriend" and at the suggestion of my first love (we had remained friends) and another close friend. I was still so very afraid of him, so when he told me that he was being discharged from the Marines (for drugs, I'd later learn), he told me to put Virginia (his home state and where he was returning) as my first choice so that I could be stationed near him. I was too afraid to tell him no, so I did what any passive-aggressive person would do, and put it down as my third choice, but told him it was my first choice.

It's funny how the Universe will make you confront that which scares you the most in order to bring you to your destiny. I got orders to go to Alaska. I was mortified! I cried and cried so much that my closest friend at that time who had been given an assignment to Langley Air Force Base in Virginia called her father, a high-ranking Army Sargent, and had my orders changed to Langley. I was now going to be an hour and a half from my "boyfriend."

A Good Man is Hard to Find

Let me step back for a moment and briefly share with you a little bit about my time in the service. I first witnessed sexual harassment and full-on domestic violence while serving my country. In basic training, the TI (Training Instructor) of the male flight made it a point to remind our female flight that women were objects for sexual pleasure, not humans. Every time we marched by them when our female TI was not with us, he'd have his flight yell out derogatory statements like "I smell tuna!" It got so bad for us that we finally broke down as a group and decided to tell our TI, TSGT Carlton.

This woman was amazing and terrifying! When I first went in to inquire about joining the service, I remember the recruiter telling me that basic training would be fine as long as I didn't get a female TI. "They were mean and vicious," he said. When I got off the bus and saw this tall, lean woman leaning against the wall with one leg, her hat tipped down to cover her eyes, I nearly freaked out. I had been assigned to one of the toughest female TI's EVER. I spent my six weeks in training praying this woman did not learn nor ever have to say my name. Of course, that did not happen. First of all, I couldn't march to save my life and tried to hide it by positioning myself in the back for our flight. That did not work! She summarily called me out: "Milbourne! You can't march for shit!" And she put me in the middle of the pack to hide that fact. 😊

But I was also one of the women instrumental in bringing to her attention the male flight's abusive behavior. It was a tough day, that day. We all gathered in the recreation room and told her what was happening. I'll never forget the look on her face or her anger at us for not having told her sooner.

The next day, the male TI was gone, and the male flight never said another word to us again. We respected TSGT Carlton more than ever after that. It was the first time many of us learned that women could be more powerful than men, and that the military was not immune to sexual harassment or assault and abuse.

When I was stationed at my permanent duty station at Langley Air Force Base in 1994, one of my closest friends became involved with a Staff Sargent, which was fraternization and against the Uniform Code of Military Justice (UCMJ). Now, fraternizing between airmen and senior ranking enlisted and officers is/was not allowed, but it happens(ed) more often than is/was made public. I soon found out that he had begun physically abusing her.

Anytime new female airmen arrived on a base, they were referred to as "fresh meat," and she and I were that. This man chased my friend until she gave in and then the control and abuse began. I was a witness to most of it. One day, he hit her in the hallway at work during a lunch break. I saw him do it and convinced my friend to report it with me. We did, and our supervisors dismissed it. They said he was a "good" Sargent and would never do something like that. It was devastating to both her and me.

Let me be very clear here. I do not regret my time in the service. I am proud to have served my country. Quite honestly, I never knew how strong I could be and what I would and would not tolerate from people in the business world until I joined. Professionalism is EVERYTHING! I left the Air Force with eight medals for my service. I was accepted in the Army's ROTC officer program at Hampton University, but declined the offer because, well, I wanted to be an English teacher. The people I served with were awesome, but there's a dark side to my experience in the military that I will never forget. It's shaped my writing (currently working on a military YV drama series), the organizations I support and my attitude about leadership and service to others. Still, I am an Airman for life, and I'm proud of it.

My Lips are Sealed

Here's another dark thing I learned from my military experience and in finding a way to escape my Marine "boyfriend:" be silent. Don't tell anyone what's happening because they won't believe you. In that, I also learned to be silent about who I was and what I wanted in a partner and in life because the man wouldn't want me if he knew the "real' me. By the time I met the man who would become my husband, I had silenced myself. I had created a representative to stand in for me in my relationships … if I chose to have one. This representative didn't talk back. She didn't share my fears or the full picture of my dreams. She held back on my thoughts about what was going on in the world, what I really wanted out of life and more importantly, she held back on my beliefs about God. Oh, my lips were sealed!

Sadly, many of us are sending our representatives to the dates and to the wedding. We've created a false persona, mostly out of pain and rejection, to be an image to the world that we've been told the world wants. When my soon to be ex-husband and I were dating, I'd listen silently as he spoke of things that were in direct contradiction to what I believed and knew to be true, but because I did not want to lose this "good" man, because we all know that a good man is hard to find, I remained silent. In my head, I screamed out all kinds of retorts to comments that he'd make or things I'd see him do that I did not agree with, but they rarely ever came out of my mouth. My reasoning was that I wasn't going to marry this person, so why tell them what I really think. Why tell him who I really am? He was showing me who he was, but I was not returning the favor. I was too afraid. My past experiences had marked me. There was no way I was going to let him in. I was going to let my representative date him.

And then I fell in love. My representative was NOT happy because I fired her right after the wedding and the "real" me showed up … with lots of baggage. The first seven years of my marriage were HORRIBLE because of this. I had opinions and was more than willing to express them now. I refused to give up my dreams of being a writer and a tenured college professor with a Ph.D. I fought hard to not only keep those dreams, but to try and make them come true. I worked as an adjunct in local colleges and universities for years much to his disdain. He did not sign up for a wife who quit teaching public school (a steady, contracted gig) to start a magazine and work as an adjunct professor, i.e., making no money. No! My representative tricked him.

My rep only told him that after I got out of the military, I was going to be a teacher. Who wouldn't think a "contracted" teacher!? But I had no intentions of teaching public school forever. I wanted to be a college professor.

I take full ownership of the role I played in my relationship. Because I had learned to be silent about who I was and what I wanted from my past relationships, I didn't tell him the truth. Let me go deeper. Because I did not tell him about my deep faith in God, when I was called to be a writer - to focus on that, to obey Him - I set both him and me up. We were unequally "yoked" and I knew it. He had told me while we were dating that he did not believe in "God," and what did I do? In my arrogance, I said to myself that if he stayed around me for long, he would. Here's the stinging truth. Scripture says to watch the company you keep because you will not wear off on them; they will wear off on you (Proverbs 13:20, GNT).

But because I had not the courage to be who I knew myself to be, and because I did not want to lose this "good" man, I sent my representative to the relationship instead of ME. To further endanger myself, I also ignored the red flags which waved brightly in the wind. I'll talk more about those red flags in the next chapter.

5 Way to Identify the "Real" You vs. the Representative in Your Relationship

1. You "speak up" when your date or partner does/says something that goes against your values and/or morals
2. You are transparent with what you will or will not accept in a relationship
3. You practice what you preach even when no one is looking
4. You do not "settle" for any man (or woman) because you're lonely
5. You're not ashamed or silenced into not talking about your faith/spirituality

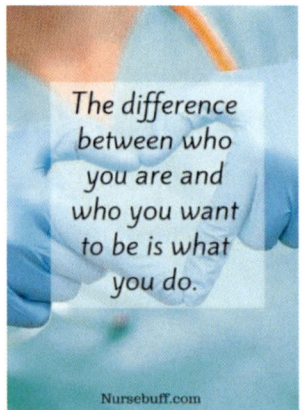

Post from 10/16/2018

What I want to be requires action. There's a reason why the scriptures say that the Divine - God - is the Great I Am. There's infinite power in proclaiming that which you know yourself to be. You were born in love to love, and love is an energy that moves the Universe. Thus, You are Love. You are able to create through this power source because you ARE the energy. Own this knowledge. Take action! Who do you want to be?! #takeactiontuesday #ILoveMeMore #IAm

Homework

Reflect back on a time in your past relationships (platonic and romantic) where you sent your representative to the date/relationship. Why do you think you were not able to bring your true self to the table? Reflecting on your current relationships, are you *You*?

Chapter 2 ~ The Red Flag Syndrome

"Sometimes what is meant for you can't find you simply because you aren't being yourself"
(Maryam Hasnaa).

Red flags are warning signs. Maya Angelou once said that when people show you who you are the first time, believe them. My college "boyfriend" was covered in red flags. First, he was an alcoholic. Every time I saw him, he was drinking. He'd get so drunk, he'd sit in a chair and just glare at everyone. He was quiet and when he did get you in his sights, he'd start to pick at everything he thought was wrong with you.

"You're fucking stupid!"

"What the fuck is wrong with you?"

Then, he'd grab me by my upper arm and squeeze it so hard, I'd start to cry.

And then there was the drugs. He smoked weed (and God only knows what else) and he was still active duty. This man did not follow the rules, and I lived my life around following the rules. So here I was with someone who was not on the same wavelength with me, the red flags were blowing wildly in the wind and I stayed.

Then I met his family upon my arrival at Langley Air Force Base in Virginia in 1994. He had been dishonorably discharged for the drug usage and went back home to Richmond. They lived in an old house in North Richmond. The house was dark and cluttered. I thought everyone must have smoked weed too because they looked high; no one wanted to look me in the eyes when he introduced me. I could not shake this feeling that I was walking into a trap. They were cold people and I began see why he was the way he was. He had no job and no career aspirations to speak of, or at least that I knew about. My spirit said "Run!" He was going to try to do to me what I saw happen to many service members: get me to marry him so that he would have benefits.

I was 21 years old. There was no way I was ready for marriage, and especially not with a man who had sabotaged his own career. And even more so, he had violated me. He never apologized or even acknowledged what he did to me that night in my apartment. As I walked back to my car, I knew I was never going to call or see him again, and I didn't. I had ignored those red flags for well over two years: too long.

I wish I could say I learned my lesson and continued to pay attention to the red flags in every relationship after this boyfriend, but I did not. In fact, I ran right into another pit of red flags that would hold me in bondage for 23 years. Again, I saw the red flags waving furiously in the wind, but I pretended not to see them.

My husband and I did have a few things in common on the surface. We both came from broken families; we poor grew up "poor" with mothers who struggled to provide for their families while the fathers went on to live their lives with the "next" wife. So, we both knew what it felt like to be abandoned as teens/pre-teens, we were both the oldest of our siblings and we both did not want to repeat the cycle of abandonment, addiction and depression. Finally, we both wanted the best for our lives. We just took different roads to achieve that dream.

Now here is where we differed tremendously and what would cause a deep riff in our marriage. As I mentioned earlier, I grew up in church and believed in God; he did not as I previously mentioned. I believed in service to others; he did not. I believed in spare the rod, spoil the child; he did not. He believed in money and power; I ran from it. I believed that love conquered all and was the guiding force in a relationship; he did not.

The first time he called me a "bitch," our son was maybe a month or two old. We had gotten into an argument about money. I was on maternity leave from my high school teaching job and money was tight. I had also had an emergency C-section and the bill for that was through the roof. I knew that he took money very seriously, but I had no idea HOW serious. It turns out, his whole identity was wrapped up in it. Now, it is a fact that men's egos are tied to their ability to provide for their families. They see their worth as being able to provide security and safety. But I did not really know this at the time. I was only 29 years old. All I knew was that the man I had married and professed to love had called me out my name like I was a trick on the street. And what made this all so much worse was the sound of his voice when he said it and the look in his eyes. He hated me.

I got into my car and drove around in the rain with my son in the backseat in his car seat. I called my mom who was living in California at the time and told her what happened. She wanted me to leave and come home, but I told her that I couldn't because I had no money. I told her that he was under a lot of stress and that maybe this was the first and last time that he would call me that.

Nope! A year or so later, we were sitting in the car in a Walmart parking lot in North Carolina. It was raining again and was late in the evening. Our son, niece and another child were in the backseat. Once again, the argument was about money and the fact that I did not have any to purchase what he wanted. He told me to "shut the fuck up" and again called me a "bitch." I was speechless and started to cry. I could not believe that he had called me that again and in front of the children. I wanted to leave and take a train or bus back home, but I was stuck there with him and his family because I had no money to leave. I was so devastated.

In January 2003, my cousin, Damita Oglesby, was tracked down by her estranged boyfriend and the father of the child she was carrying and stabbed in the head with a screwdriver. It was one of the cruelest attacks I'd ever heard. She had a restraining/protective order against him, and had even moved to Atlanta, GA from New Jersey to start over, but he still found her and killed her. She lived in a coma until May when they delivered her last baby. She died soon after turning 30, leaving behind seven children. I was in Hawaii presenting a paper I had written in graduate school at a humanities conference at the University of Hawaii. My husband was with me, although he came begrudgingly because he didn't think we could afford to go and that I was just chasing a worthless dream.

When I got that call, I remember thinking that I had to do something about this. I did not want to see another woman suffer at the hands of her abuser, but I didn't know exactly what I could do. And when she died, in prayer, I asked God to show me what He needed me to do. From that prayer came something amazing.

Now let me step back for a moment. I had just been hired to be the Director of Education for a small for-profit allied health school. I was going to be making $45,000 a year, the most money I had ever made. My husband was ecstatic because he felt that my master's degree was now coming in handy and was going to pay for itself. Never mind the fact that I pretty much earned my MA by myself because he had often refused to watch our newborn son when I had to work on class assignments. He also believed that the financial burden of taking care of a wife, a toddler and our first home would be relieved because now I could pay half of everything.

On the morning that I prayed to God for Him to use me, I went to work and was summarily fired. I had never been fired from a job in my life! Instead of crying about it, though, I smiled as I packed my stuff from my office because: 1) God has a serious sense of humor and 2) He had given me a new calling. A week later, a month after my cousin's death, I launched a motivational magazine for women called *Average Girl Magazine*. Its mission was to empower and uplift women ages 25-55 through articles on health and wellness, financial information for your business and personal and spiritual growth and awareness.

What began as a two page newsletter eventually became a 64-page full-colored magazine for women. I was determined to save another woman's life and I dedicated the magazine and every speaking engagement I had as a result of it to Damita. But what I didn't share too often because I had pushed it deep into the back of my mind was that her story was *my* story.

My marriage was not a happy one. I was being emotionally abused. He did not support the magazine because it took the money I had earned as an adjunct teaching or other part-time jobs from the household - or so he thought. I rarely ever used my own money to fund my business. I used "other people's money":

advertisers, sponsors, vendors, etc. But he refused to believe that. So, his animosity towards me grew. And my silence deepened to the point where my family began to notice a significant change in me. They could not understand why I was not fighting back hard enough. Where was "Evil Lynn"?

She was gone … for good. And it was my fault. My marriage was suffocating from a disease called silence. The silence I had maintained while we were dating had grown like a cancer. I just could not fully bring myself to speak up. Instead, I was passive aggressive. I would do things behind his back like create events and take on teaching jobs that I knew did not pay what he wanted me to make. He thought because I had a master's degree that meant I should be working in corporate America making a big salary. I was not going to do that, but I didn't tell him at first and that was where I was wrong.

When we first met, I was in the military and was making decent money for a 23-year old. I told him that I wanted to be a teacher, and that I was going back to school for it. So, when we began dating, I was making decent money. But here's the thing: he paid for nearly everything when we were dating. I never had to worry about anything. Although I was making decent money,

I never got to keep any of it because I was in a lot of debt. I had never really been taught how to manage money (perhaps because we lived from paycheck to paycheck). I was also now sharing a pretty expensive apartment with my sister and brother who had made their way to Virginia from California to live with me. I had bought a car that cost too much money and wasn't even worth it (it was a lemon), so I had to get another car and was now upside down. In short, my personal debt was high. But for the first time in my life, I didn't have to worry about paying for trips or eating out necessarily because I had a man who took care of me when we were together. Or so I thought.

What I would come to realize is that *his* representative was setting me up. He had me to believe that this person loved to take care of me (security), would provide for me and would support me. But here's where my representative got in the way. She didn't share the full depth of her dreams or finances because she had both of us believing that the relationship was not going to go into marriage, so why say anything. Remember, when he told me that he didn't believe in God, I remained silent. When he told me that the homeless man standing on the corner asking for money to get food was a liar and should "just go get a job," I said nothing. When we saw a man getting beat up in the street, he acted like he didn't see anything and kept driving. I said nothing. When he *told* me we should get married but did not get down on one knee to ask me (which I really wanted, but did not have the courage to ask), I agreed. His representative told me other stories that I won't share here because it would hurt my children and our very fragile relationship as it stands now. But they were all red flags that I chose not to see.

Why did I choose to ignore these things? Because I was afraid and unsure of myself. I did not want my marriage to fail; I didn't think that I could make it on my own. My dad had told me I wasn't going to be anything, and I was determined to prove him wrong. And I was in love. Or at least that is what I thought.

I had these same excuses the first time I left my husband in 2009 after he tried to choke me during yet another argument about money. I had my then two-month old daughter in my arms and when he pushed me down on the bed, she flew out of my arms landing only a few inches from me on the bed. My son and niece were in the living room and all I could think about as I watched him pull back his arm and ball his hand into a fist, was that I was not going to make it. My kids were going to lose their mother. I thought about Damita and her death.

I screamed his name loudly enough that he came to his senses before hitting me with his fist, but his other hand still had a hold of my throat. He eventually let it go and I was able to get my daughter, and after begging him to give me back my cell phone, I called the police. And would you believe that he went to the police and pressed charges against *me* for assault? I had choke marks on my neck, but I had to go to the county jail and turn myself in for "assaulting" him, even though I had put my hands out in self-defense, and he knew that. But abusers know how to use the law against their victims. When we went to court, I had to make a deal in order not to be charged with assault.

I wish I could tell you that I learned my lesson and left him alone for good. I used to say what a lot of women say before they find themselves in an abusive relationship:

I'll never go back to a man if he hits me.
Girl, I'd get a knife and kill him.

Nope! My abusive ex-boyfriend had trained me well. I left my marriage and moved into my own place, but six months later, I took my husband back. Why? Because of what I said earlier: fear. I kept hearing my dad say I was never going to be anything and my ex-boyfriend calling me stupid.

When I left, I had no money or credit to my name. And to make matters worse, because I made too much money as a teacher (even though I was on maternity leave), I couldn't even qualify for food stamps or other services, but God had me. I was able to get a two-bedroom apartment in the best part of town and the few people I told what happened, blessed me with money for the deposit and first month's rent on the apartment. I was able to get the cable and water connected and the electricity turned on. Yet, even with all this proof of God's favor, I panicked and let myself be talked into going back to my marriage.

And the day I agreed to do so, I knew it was a mistake that I would pay for. I had hoped things would change. We went to counseling for a minute, but he refused to go back, which was part of the agreement for reconciliation. I had violated the one-year protective order I had against him for the assault by taking him back. Nothing he promised to do to help mend the marriage did he do. For years, I endured him swearing that I begged him to come back to me and that I couldn't make it without him. For years, I tried to find my voice through my writings and even in the business of *Average Girl Magazine* and another business I would start in 2014, The Pierce Agency, but nothing seemed to work out for me. I felt trapped and alone, but even more deadly for me and my children, I stayed silent …again. Here I was encouraging other women to find their voices and to live their lives on purpose, but I was lying and hiding the truth of my existence. I began to feel like the biggest fraud in the world. And worse, deep down inside, I knew I was being used.

Post 1/7/2019

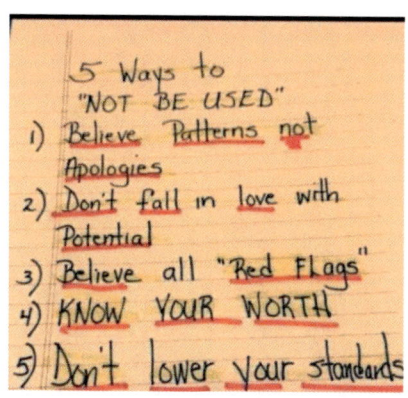

"5 Ways Not to Be Used"

"I'm guilty of doing all five of the things on this list and I paid a heavy price for it. But here's the thing that can save both me and you a lot of heartache, time lost and opportunities: step #4. If you know AND CLAIM your worth, the other steps won't be necessary because they will have never happened. #motivationmonday #ILoveMeMore

Homework

Which one of these rules have you broken the most? Why have you done so? What are two things you can do today to begin to change this?

Chapter 3 ~ Silence is the Death of Strength

"Silence speaks a thousand words" (Unknown).

In mid-2017, after another explosive argument about my lack of a *real* income between my husband and I, my son came to me. We were in the kitchen and he said, "I don't know how you do it, mom. You're so strong. I would have left a long time ago."

I was devastated. I remember replying, "Maybe the strength isn't in the staying, but in the leaving, son." I cried hard. I knew then and there that I had to make a change. My son was witnessing the withstanding of verbal attacks as strength. "Taking it" is not strength. I was not teaching my children strength. I was teaching them silence.

No one outside of my sister and mother knew how bad things were in my marriage. No one knew that the kids were witnessing violent arguments and attacks where their mother was being brutally cussed out and crushed spiritually and emotionally. And no one knew because they were made to believe that this type of environment was "normal." Whereas I would hold onto the pain and anger of the argument for days and weeks, even not speaking to him for months, their father would immediately act like things were back to normal. This was NOT normal!

I had started *Average Girl Magazine* in 2003 with the intention of saving the lives of women in abusive relationships. By 2009/10, the stress of trying to act like I could handle everything was taking its toll on my mind, body and soul. My business was not doing so well, I was 50 pounds overweight and my husband and I had finally confronted the fact that we didn't like each other very much. He said I had changed. That I was not who he thought he had married, and guess what? He was right! I had been called to publish the magazine and thus had stopped looking for full-time work so that I could run my company. I was teaching English part-time and working on my business the other time. He hated that because our finances were tight and I refused to let go of the magazine.

But I made a huge mistake, which added to the stress. I had assumed that I was supposed to make money in this business. When I first started the magazine, no one I talked to could tell me how to start because the truth is, they had all come on board after the publications they worked for had already been successfully operating for years. These men (there were no women doing what I was doing then) told me I'd never succeed. That no one would buy my magazine, and I heard this at home, too. Tto prove all of them wrong, I put my vision onto the magazine. I had pushed God's vision and plan aside to boost my ego. I realized this one day when I was talking to a friend, complaining about how the publication was in the red because I sucked at selling advertising. She responded, "Who told you that it was supposed to make money?" Yes, who told me? Me!

In trying to prove I was smart enough and good enough to create a successful business, I lost sight of the calling. I pushed that magazine from a two-page newsletter to a 64-page full colored glossy magazine with a distribution of over 5,000 copies up and down the Mid-Atlantic region. I hosted workshops and seminars for women in my city featuring international speakers such as Susan B. Taylor of *Essence Magazine* and Kim Coles and Daphne Maxwell Reid, Hollywood actresses and authors.

To the world, I looked like I had things in check and was successful, but I was operating from a belief system that I had something to prove to my husband, to my father, to men who told me I was nothing. I had produced my own plays and films with "other people's money" because everyone thought I had it all together. I did not. I was actually fighting (but really running from) a lie. I believed it enough to put my health, sanity and finances at risk of exploding in my face. And they did!

By the time my son and I got to that scene in the kitchen in early 2017, I was broken physically, emotionally, financially and spiritually. I'd started two new businesses since 2014: The Pierce Agency, LLC and RLP Productions. Both companies were founded with the purpose to help people bring their stories (non-fiction, fiction) to the publishing or entertainment world. I felt that, again, I was being called to use my gifts to help people follow their dreams. But I hit yet another issue that I continued to avoid: valuing myself.

My problem was that I could not bring myself to charge appropriately for my services because I felt like I was not worth it. I was crippled by my fear of value and lack. I was being torn down at home because I did not make enough of money, my father had left my mother because she did not have it and I pursued a career where you weren't paid hardly enough for the hours and energy put into it: teaching. My entire perception of money was warped. I was being told from almost every area in my life that I was "nothing" without it, and thus, I ran like hell from it.

I have been ripped off and underpaid, and it wasn't because I was stupid or didn't understand money. It was because I did not speak up and know my worth. So, the silence I was hiding behind involved more than just my marriage; it involved my entire life. I'd go to the store determined to buy myself something that I needed, and I'd find myself standing in the aisle arguing with myself about whether or not I really should buy the item: a cheap pair of earrings, a notebook, a pair of shoes. I once spent an hour in the purse section of JC Penny's asking my eight-year-old daughter if I should really buy a Calvin Klein purse. It was so bad, my daughter finally *demanded* I get in the line and buy the thing.

Why could I not bring myself to spend money on myself? My money? Because anything I bought for me, I was going to hear about it eventually. I was going to be questioned about the money and where it came from. He was going to tell me that I was being selfish and should have given him that money to pay for our kids' this or that or the cable bill or the rent. Yes, he demanded that I at least pay half of the rent because marriage is a partnership, he said. I was giving him just about everything I had because I felt guilty and pressured.

Now I knew that this was not what I had been taught nor believed about a marriage. The *Bible* says that "He who finds a true and faithful wife finds a good thing" (Proverbs 18:22, AMP). I was not his "good thing." I was a "partner," not a wife. I was raised to believe that the man is the head of the household. The wife is to submit to him, meaning she has his back and is there for him when he needs her. NOT, that she is to be the head of the house and provide for a man. Not that she is to relinquish everything to him. Again, because I did not ask questions about his beliefs about marriage (and other things that were important to me), I found myself in a relationship where I was not a "good thing." I was a financial pack mule.

So, if I did buy something for myself, I hid it in the trunk of my car until I could sneak it in the house and into my closet - too scared and ashamed to bring it into the house in full sight of family. No wonder I couldn't place a value - worthiness - on my gifts or me. No wonder I was lost to silence. Quite honestly, it felt as if I never even stood a chance. My mentality was one of lack. I had been operating from a place of lack all my life, and the environment that I was living in, worked to keep me down and in a place of unworthiness. But only because I allowed it to.

Here's the thing: a spirit of lacking means that you have no faith. I remember when my son was about five-years-old and he was constantly wanting to build a skateboard ramp to jump off. Each time he'd ask me if he could, I'd say no, and I said no because we did not have health insurance. I made the mistake of telling this to my son each and every time he asked me if he could ride the skateboard or make a ramp. One day, he tried it one more time, but before I could answer him, he said, "I know, I know. We don't have any health insurance." And then he walked away, defeated.

When he was seven and eight, he asked me if he could make a lemonade stand and sell lemonade for the summer. I told him no both times because I said I didn't have the money to buy the supplies. I didn't even attempt to buy them, though. I just said we didn't have any money. I was projecting onto him my spirit of lack - fear. I was afraid to even try because in the back of my mind, I kept hearing 'I'll never get that money back if I spend what little I have.' I heard, 'he's a dreamer like you, and your dreams have never worked out.' I shut him down because I was afraid: of failing, of not having, of what his father would say. I was afraid to hear – and for him to hear – that I/he was nothing.

I was always afraid of what my husband would say. Yes, I started three businesses during my marriage, but none of them were successful financially because I was afraid: of money, of my husband's thoughts and other people's thoughts about me. This was lack at work. I believed in all these thoughts. These things born of fear, and because I believed in them, that meant I did not believe in Him.

God has had my back all my life. He has protected me and provided for me when there seemed to be no way. I produced my plays and films as I said earlier with "other people's" money, but it was the grace of God who put it on their hearts to bless me with the funds to do what I did. I've traveled to Europe and NY and CA and other cities with favor because I had no means to go to these places, but God did. He had the means and the way if only I would believe, have faith and put in the work. And deep inside I knew all of this to be true because when I did break through the silence, He showed me His grace and promise to me. But when I allowed my fears to get in the way of keeping my heart and soul connected to him, I suffered. And so did my children.

Post from 12/28/2018

One of the boldest and greatest changes I made to my life's story after I left my volatile and abusive marriage one year and one month ago was to become the leading lady in my own story. That meant, however, that I had to confront the part that I played in the tearing down of my self-esteem. I believed the lie that I was a nobody and that I couldn't make it on my own. That love was not for me. It was all a story fear had created for me and I lived it - believed it - for all of my teen, young adult and adult life. Until now! I am worthy of love, joy, prosperity and happiness. This is my new story and I'm going to tell it wherever I go for the rest of my life. I hope you'll join me. Let's create a new story for ourselves. Let's be fearless! Who's with me? #fearlessfriday #ILoveMeMore

Homework

What stories are you telling yourself that do not truly reflect who you are? How has the spirit of "lack" affected your ability to tell your story?

Chapter 4 ~ In Search of Love

"There is no fear in love; but perfect love casteth out fear: because fear hath torment" (1 John 4:18, KJV).

I have always longed for love. I grew up with my nose in a book, and not just *any* book. Three kinds: mysteries, westerns and romances. Agatha Christie, Louie Lamar and Harlequin Romance were my favorites. I used to get in trouble with my mom because whenever she needed me to do something, I could never hear her calling me because I had my nose in a book. By the time I went to college, I had amassed a collection of these books, but particularly, the romances.

Maybe it's the artist in me, but I am drawn to love stories or at least I was. Reading about people from different backgrounds and lives, meeting and then going through adversity to find and then love one another was so appealing to me. I longed to know what it was like to have someone love me for who I was even as young as 12. Perhaps because I had learned early that love hurt. I saw my mother be rejected by the man who claimed to love her. My father abandoned our family for other women who had more than my mother - or me. This constant stream of rejection threaded itself throughout my life and relationships, so it was in books where I escaped from my reality.

My favorite book when I was about 13 or so was *Are You There God! It's Me, Margaret*, by Judy Blume. Talk about a coming of age story! Margaret longs to have breasts and physical beauty, and so she and her friends create "beauty" rituals to try and do so. In one scene, Margret repeats the following mantra while squeezing her arms into her chest: "I must, I must, I must increase my bust" was one of the funniest and saddest scenes in the book. Funny, because I already had a size 36 C cup at 13, and sad because, well, I already wore a 36 C cup by 13. My menstrual cycle started when I was 10, and so I was already where Margaret wanted to be physically, but unlike Margaret, I was not "pretty."

As I said before, I was knock-kneed, had extremely thick hair that grew out, not down. I wore glasses which I sometimes had to tape on the nose bridge because I broke them often and we didn't have the money to get a new pair right away and my teeth were crooked. I was not exactly what boys wanted, I thought. It didn't help that at the time, there was a commercial for contact lenses: "girls who wear glasses do not get boyfriends." Talk about crushing a girl's self-esteem. So, boys did not look my way … but men did.

Predators are Everywhere!

When I was 14, we lived with my mother's boyfriend at the time. He had offered his home to us as we had been homeless, living from friend's house to friend's house. He had a son we shall call Robert. Robert was 24 years old. He took a liking to me which I found exciting, but scary at the same time. He looked at me in a way that sent tingles coursing through my body, a feeling I was not familiar with. Soon, I found myself alone with him, too.

Predators are everywhere. Robert knew that I was a young and naive, but more than anything, I was vulnerable. There was no father around to protect me and because we had no home of our own, we were somewhat beholden to *his* father for giving us a place to live. He would tell my mom that he was taking me with him to the store, but instead, he would drive me to a secluded location and fondle me. Like many predators, he put me at ease by saying, "If you don't want me to touch you, I won't." He made me think I was in control when the truth was, he was.

When I look back on this moment in my life, I realize that he was grooming me. Thankfully, my instincts were strong, and I never let him go too far with me. I was too afraid to have sex with him because 1) I was a virgin, and remember those romance novels I told you I read? I had envisioned my first time being with someone I loved in a romantic setting, not in the backseat of a truck; 2) I knew instinctively that this was wrong. A grown man was touching me and had my mother and others believing he was "cool." And here's the thing: I really liked it and him. In fact, I desperately wanted someone to like me. Again, I was, in my opinion, an ugly, awkward, bottle-coke glasses wearing little girl. I had large breasts and a small waist, but when I looked in the mirror, I saw ugliness. I saw that I was fat and a nothing. After all, that is what my father had told me. Robert said everything I wanted to hear. He made me feel desired, but my instincts were much stronger than my desires.

This went on for several months until one day, when I came home from school, my mother had our things packed and told us we were leaving. And we did. My mother had found a run-down house a few blocks away for rent. The house had no working heat and had been empty for years. No one should have been living in that place (years later, it would be officially condemned), but my mom had been desperate to get away from her boyfriend. At the time, I had no idea why we had left in such a hurry and under what circumstances until well into adulthood. It turns out that while Robert was "grooming" me, his father had his eyes on my 13-year-old sister. A few days prior to leaving, he had asked my mom for my sister. This "man" wanted to have sex with a child. Both men! My mother literally took us and ran.

    I wish that I could say that this was the last time a man would ask for me or my sister, but it wasn't. These men thought that because my mother was struggling to provide for four children, she would sacrifice her daughters. They didn't know my mother. She had pleaded the blood of Jesus over her children, and she would rather sleep in her car with us, live in a homeless shelter or in a run down, condemned home before she let anyone hurt us.

    When I was 16, I met my first boyfriend, "Sam." He was one of the most intelligent, yet weirdest boy I had ever met. He was an aspiring artist and designer. He went to a different high school than me, but because our parents were friends, we saw each other often. Sam was extremely quiet and standoffish. When he asked me to be his girlfriend, I think I said yes more so because his parents liked me and desperately wanted me to like their son than I had feelings for him. And I, quite frankly, I was happy that someone finally liked me. I remember when I was in the 5th grade and a boy (also named John) in my class found out that I liked him. He laughed at me and made fun of me after that. I was terrified and humiliated. Every boy I liked did not even see me, let alone liked me back. So, when Same came along, I was ready and happy … For a minute.

Something was not right with Sam. He was too quiet. His step-dad was overly aggressive about people liking his son, and when he drank, he became verbally aggressive towards everyone, but especially Sam. I could not understand it because he was so smart and creative. He could draw and paint just like his step-dad, and he loved music. He wore a mohawk, something no black boy I knew wore back then. Sam and I didn't last very long. He wanted to be my "first," but, again, something told me not to go there. He was emotionally unhinged at times; he'd get angry about something and go completely off, and then stop and get *really* quiet. I was scared. He scared me.

I found out many years later that he'd had a nervous breakdown. He'd been keeping a dark secret that was only revealed to me after his mother died of cancer. His step-father had been molesting him since he was a little boy, right after he had married Sam's mother. It explained so much about his odd behavior when we were 16. It also explained his step-father's obsession with him dating girls. He wanted to deflect from what he was doing to Sam, I believe. Again, my mother sensing that something was not right with this family, had long stopped being friends with them and made sure I did not have much interaction with Sam after we broke up, even though I did not know why at the time. But I was more than happy to stay away. College gave me a great excuse to leave town and John.

Looking back on that experience, I grieve for the little boy that was keeping such a big secret. His truth came out in his behavior, but, again, I was too young to understand on a conscious level. And in the beginning of our relationship, I was willing to ignore the red flags because I wanted a boy to like me, to love me.

I Wish You Weren't My Father

My dad was in and out of my life during this time. I remember when I was about to leave for college and my dad was coming over to our apartment for some reason. My parents had long since been divorced, but he felt the need to still try and tell her and us what to do. An argument ensued, and on his way out the door (again), he turned and said to me, "You'll never be anything." I cussed him out. Literally. I was so angry. He had spoken those words over my life when I was 12 and now, here he was trying to do it again at 17. I was not having it. I know that the *Bible* says to honor thy mother and father, but at that time in my life, I was so hurt and angry. I hated my father for leaving us and putting us in harm's way. I wished he were not my father.

Both of my brothers were gang-members at this time and their lives were on the edge, and here he was trying to tell me that I was never going to be anything. I said to him, "You don't even fucking know me." How could I honor a man who refused to honor his family? He was on wife number two by then with two more to go. How dare he! It was clear that all he cared about was controlling everyone and everything. He had no real desire to know who I was – or my siblings. It was about power and control, just like with Sam's father and just like with Robert and his father. Every man in my life, or around the periphery of my life, wanted nothing but power and control over me and everyone in their lives that they professed to love. Well, that's not love. Not even close.

When I became a parent, I had to make a difficult decision: to forgive my father and release the anger or hold onto it and pass it down to my son. I decided to forgive my father and release my anger because it wasn't fair or right to pass on what I felt to a child who knew nothing about what had happened. I decided to let my son find out for himself who his grandfather was, and he has. What I told my son when he was able to understand was that I had decided I would not give him my pain. That forgiveness was not for my father because he will never accept nor understand the pain he has caused not only our family, but the other wives and their families. He won't and can't own it, but that doesn't mean I have to live my life drowning in pain and sadness. No. I choose to love my father from a distance. He will not ever be in my inner circle because he is destructive to my well-being.

This is what we must all come to learn and understand. That the people who have hurt us are not in the place nor the space to hear the truth about themselves and how they've hurt us. But we cannot spend our precious lives expending energy to try and make them own their errors. That's not living, and we do great harm to ourselves and our children when we allow them to inherit our anger and pain. No ma'am. I did not bring this child here to hate. I love him and me more than that.

Post from 11/21/2018

To blossom is to be free... from everything that does not fill you with love and allow you to BE love.

#wellnesswednesday #ILoveMeMore

Homework

Take inventory of the people that are in your inner circle. Do they fill you with love and allow you to be Love? Or do they cripple you? Who needs to be removed from your inner circle and loved from a distance?

Chapter 5 ~ Boldness to be Claimed

"Freedom lies in being bold" (Robert Frost).

I remember sitting at the desk in my bedroom one moonlit night. I was staring out of the bedroom window up at the star-filled sky. My husband was downstairs watching tv. We had not spoken to one another in a few days after yet another heated argument about me not "pulling my weight." My heart was heavy because I was so unhappy; we both were. We were clearly at the end of our marriage, but it was like the Gladys Knight song: neither one of us wanted to be the first to say goodbye. In fact, I cried every time I heard that song because it was my life. I did not know how or had the courage to end this toxic and destructive behavior.

As I stared out the window, I remembered something deep inside of my heart. I wanted to be loved. I wanted to know what it was like to walk through my front door and there be someone happy to see me. I wanted to know what it was like for someone to pray for me because they understood the power of prayer, especially over your spouse and home. I wanted to know what it was like for someone to kiss me without having to beg for affection. I knew that if I stayed in this marriage for another year or 20, I'd never know what it was to be loved down to the bone. And even if I never fell in love again, I wanted to be "available" to it, if and when it came for me.

But even more so, I had to heal first. You cannot be angry and broken if you want to be open to receiving and giving love. You must begin the journey to working on loving yourself. What I learned in the first year of my separation in 2018 was that you cannot give to others what you do not have to give to yourself. One of the selfish reasons I stayed in my marriage so long was because I felt that if the light in me could love and embrace the light that was somewhere deep within my husband's heart, we could make it. Wrong!

What I came to realize at the end of my marriage was that his light was dimming mine to the point of extinguishment. And it was because he could not give to me what he was unable (or unwilling) to give to himself. Steve Harvey has told women hundreds of times over the years that if a man is not willing to change some things about himself to be with you, then you are not the one. He was right. I was not the one for my husband, and I had to accept that.

In January 2018, a few months after I left my marriage, I signed up for this course called *2018 Year of Miracles* moderated by authors Marci Shimff and Debra Poneman. The year-long course was designed to help participants create the space for miracles in their lives through changing the way we think and operate in our daily living: to move from ego-intention to soul-intention. Prior to joining this course, I had attended a white stone ceremony at a Unity church with a friend. If you've never attended one of these ceremonies, you should, because through guided meditation (prayer), one is able to tap into a guiding word or words to help them access growth and healing throughout the coming year.

Having my religious foundation in Pentecostalism, I went into this event with some reservations because this was not what I knew as "church." I had been told that meditation was not of God. Wrong, again! We each come to God in our own way, I have learned. Prayer is you telling God what you want, but meditation is listening to His answer. Scripture says to "Be still, and know that I Am" (Psalm 46:10). The stillness is silence, and mediation is all about silencing the noisy mind so that you can listen and feel.

Well, as I sat still in the silent church that New Year's day, the word that came to me during the ceremony was "boldness." When Marci and Debra took us through a similar meditation later that January, the word "boldness" came to me again. I had just made a major move in my life. I had "jumped" (I ended my marriage). Just like when I had left in 2009, I had no money, no credit, was about to lose my home and had just started a new part-time job where, although I was going to expand my teaching skills teaching ESL, the hourly salary was not going to cover even 50% of my bills. I was fresh in a bankruptcy and in debt up to my ears. How was I going to make it? My husband's salary had at least provided for most of the household bills, but now I didn't have that … by choice.

I was going to need to be bold. Bold in claiming love for myself - bold in jumping off the cliff of uncertainty. I was completely terrified, but resolute in my decision. If healing required boldness, if love required boldness, if shining my light required boldness, then that's what I was going to be: BOLD!

I had to boldly accept that, again, God was not bound by form. Everything I was going to do after the ceremony and the course was going to take bold faith to press forward when it looked like I was going to break.

But let me tell you something about brokenness. That is when God can use you. I once heard a sermon where the preacher demonstrated through parables how God sent His son, Jesus, to save the broken. Not one of the 12 disciples Jesus chose was a perfect man. Each one had done his fair share of dirt. Every person Jesus encountered on His journey and saved/healed was a broken vessel in some way. Their rise to healing required bold action: touching the hem of His garment, washing His feet with oil, going to the top of the mountain alone, leading His people out of Egypt.

I had asked God for a way out of my circumstances no matter what it looked like, and He gave it to me. I accepted and now I had to keep going in my boldness. I didn't get to complete the course in miracles because of personal reasons, but before I left it, I added a tool to my healing arsenal: daily affirmations - miracle-minded thoughts that I'd share with others each day on social media.

I've come to learn that I've lived my life by a particular pattern: self-doubt and the spirit of lack. If I was going to make it, I was going to have to live my life by a new pattern: Self-Love and Joy.

Post from 12/29/2018

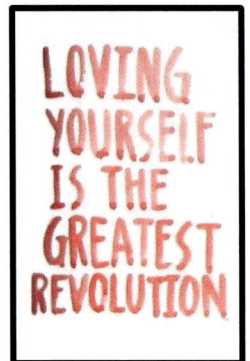

Are you ready for your revolution? I've got my sword and shield. I'm going to fight right alongside of you. ♡ #sassysaturday #ILoveMeMore #woundedwarrior #selflove #revolution

Homework

It's time to armor up! There is an attack on women and are ability to love ourselves and serve the world with love and our light. What is your sword and shield? Mine is Self-Love and Joy.

Chapter 6 ~ A Return to Joy

"Weeping may stay for the night, but rejoicing comes in the morning" (Psalm 30:5).

Grief is a powerful feeling that people often mistake for sadness, but it is much deeper than that. Looking back on my life, I see that many of my decisions regarding my career and relationships was based on grief. That is, I never fully grieved the loss of my father. He was not the greatest dad; in fact, I hardly remember anything about him prior to his leaving us. My strongest memories of him are after his departure from our lives, and it is because of the effects of his departure: homelessness, poverty, sadness, hunger, anger and words. What I was grieving was not his loss per se, but that of joy.

I believe that each of us is born with joy in our hearts. It is ingrained in us to have joy. Have you ever watched a baby's expression when they play with their favorite toy? The laughter that pours out from them as they clap their hands and squeal in delight is joy. It is not faked or manufactured. It comes from the core of existence: the heart.

I was missing joy in my life. We had spent the most formative years of our lives struggling to survive, literally. I was grieving the loss of joy because I was trapped in the vicious cycle of survival. It is hard to be joyful when you're hungry for physical nourishment and spiritual nourishment. These are blockers to creativity and communication. In other words, physiologically speaking, if your body is not receiving enough nutrition, the brain's electrical current system, the synapses, will slow down or stop the communication signals that go to the heart and the other systems of the body that keep it functioning. The part of the brain that is responsible for awareness and creativity (the right side of the brain) is crippled as is the left side of the brain, which is responsible for logic and reasoning.

Our bodies and minds need stimulation for growth and development. Food and exercise give us this; they work together to create a viable, healthy and functioning human being. They also allow us to communicate with the Divine. In the book, *Women, Food and God*, by Geneen Roth, she talks about how what we eat and when we eat it can directly affect our ability to communicate with God. You cannot hear the answer to your prayers if your ears are filled with the sounds of you munching on a bag of chips. In other words, when we allow ourselves to be consumed with negative emotions and eat in direct response to those emotions, we are putting up a wall between ourselves and our creator. The wall is packed with sugars, preservatives, steroids and all the bad stuff that causes our bodies to become obese, develop high blood pressure, diabetic, etc.

Roth argues that we must become aware of how our emotions are fueling our drive or lack thereof. In short, I was letting my emotions run my life. By the time I was in the 7th year of my marriage, I was 50 pounds overweight and felt like God had abandoned me … another father had left me. I was letting stress take over my life and it was killing me. I finally figured all of this out after I left my marriage the first time in 2009 and read Roth's book. I lost 25 pounds and was on my way to healing. I even began to experience the one emotion-feeling that I believed had alluded me all these years: joy.

I was so open and aware of what I was feeling and eating in response to those feelings that I created a presentation (followed up by a book) called *Kryptonite Killed Superwoman: Turning in the Cape for an Authentic Purpose-Driven Life* in 2012. The book featured articles and blogs I had written since 2004 about my marriage, being a mother and an entrepreneur. And contained within each piece was the truth of my existence ... sort of. I had come to understand something very important about being a modern woman: I was putting everyone's needs before for myself. As Iyanla Vanzant had once told in an interview she did for *Average Girl Magazine,* I was *giving* my joy away. And I was doing that because I was trying to rescue everyone except myself. Sound familiar?

    The phrase "Superwoman" is used to describe the woman who does it all. It was intended to be a sort of badge of honor, but I have come to despise it. I was learning that this "superwoman" was dying of kryptonite poisoning. In the presentation, I describe "Kryptonite" as being anything or anyone that distracts you from taking care of you to the point of losing one's identity and sense of self - an unhealthy obsession: work, church, family, sex, substance abuse, shopping. Do you know what the number one killer of women is? Heart disease. Ironic, isn't it? Women are emotional creatures. We care about people and will give just about anything to help someone in need. We are wired to be multi-taskers. We are wired to birth and care for others.

Our hearts are big. No wonder it is the very thing that kills us.

I wish that I could say that I took my own advice in my book. I didn't. In fact, by the end of 2012, I had been back with my husband for almost two years by then. I had gained back the 25 plus pounds I had shed and felt lost more than ever. I felt like a fraud publishing the book and presentation because here I was back where I had started: in an emotionally abusive relationship.

I was clinging to what joy I had left. I was so unhappy and lost. I knew deep within my bones and heart that I was living a lie and that I needed to find my way out of the hell that I had put myself in. How could I be telling women to love themselves if I could not do it myself? I have this saying: pretty on the outside, broken on the inside. That was me. To my friends, family and followers on social media, I looked like I had it together, but it was not true, and if you read *Kryptonite Killed Superwoman* closely, you'd have seen that I was the complete and total opposite.

Every time I gave this presentation, referred Geneen's Roth's book and showed up for book signings, I fought back tears because although I believed wholeheartedly that I was not made to be someone's mule, I had not yet the courage to leave the relationship - to reclaim joy. As I stated before, I was not yet ready to let go emotionally. I had not hit emotional bankruptcy yet. And this the problem for many women (and men) in abusive relationships. You're not ready to break the emotional chain.

It wasn't until he punched a hole in our bedroom wall instead of my face on Christmas Eve 2016 that I was finally, officially done. Once again, we had argued about money, but this time, my mother and sister were witnesses to our volatile and destructive relationship. All I had wanted to do that day was wrap Christmas gifts with my sister (we spent every Christmas together with our families) in my room, but he didn't want me to. He hated my sister for being vocal about how he treated me. She was not someone he could walk over or shut up, so he was never happy whenever she was around.

Tensions exploded. I had finally had enough and lost it. My mother and sister had to physically pull me away from him because I had gotten in his face and was going to let what would be, be. I had snapped. In response, he punched a hole in the wall by our bedroom door right where I had stood seconds before. I had no doubt, then or now, that he really wanted to punch me instead of that wall.

A few minutes later, my son and I went to the store, and I remember telling him then that I had had enough and that we were going to leave soon. In my head and heart, I was finally done unlike in 2009 when we first separated. Then, I let fear stop me from staying separated again. And it was able to do that because I was not emotionally done by then. Now, on Christmas Eve 2016, I was. I knew that if I did not leave soon, it was not going to end well for me emotionally, physically, spiritually or financially, and truth be told, it already wasn't going well for me in any of those areas in my life.

I wanted joy instead of pain. I wanted to love and be loved freely. I wanted my children to know what is was to live without impending violence. I chose the man I married (and all the other men I dated) because I had not fully grieved the loss of my father in my life. My mother didn't put me or my siblings in therapy because that didn't really exist back then. And she could not have afforded it if it did, not with four kids in need.

I went through my formative years grieving, and that was expressed through anger and isolation. I didn't have a lot of friends because I kept to myself. I kept my nose in a book. But this is what made me a target for older men like "Robert." I oozed fatherlessness. I dripped abandonment.

So, I was unable to process my grief healthily, and as a result, I went looking for my father in the men I encountered. I was an easy target for predators in my teens and young adulthood. I had learned early that if you wanted to keep a man, you didn't let him know the real you. But here's the sad part, I didn't know the real me either. And that's how I found myself in the car that Christmas Eve telling my then 13-year-old son that we were going to leave one day soon. Where I finally found myself telling God, "I don't care how you get me out of this marriage, just please make a way."

The experts talk about having an Exit Plan when leaving an abusive marriage. I disagree with this for one reason only: it won't work if you are not emotionally ready to end the relationship. When you are finally emotionally bankrupt, when you finally tell God, the Divine, "I'm ready. I don't care what my escape looks like. Just get me out," the universe springs into action. Yes, have someplace to go and money to provide for yourself if you can. But one must be ready emotionally to leave. I knew, this time, that all I needed to do was to open my eyes and watch and wait. Joy (freedom) was calling me and this time, I answered.

All my life, I hid my fears behind a false sense of bravado. I put on the mask and never took it off. But the thing about being a writer, is that the truth of who you are always comes out in the writing. One of the first writing assignments I used to give my students was to write an essay about themselves and I'd warn them about making stuff up or holding back because the writing would tell me the truth. It's in the words you choose to use, their placement within the sentence and the tone. Tone is always present in the writing. And guess what? I could always spot the lie.

And that's why I am writing this book today. Every time I created a presentation for a woman's group or wrote a blog, my truth haunted me. Not one presentation or book or blog hid me. The truth was always there and if you have ever heard me speak or read any of my inspirational blogs/articles, you felt it. I was letting pieces of myself come through. You felt it but couldn't put a name to it - what you were feeling. But you knew it was there because it was in you, too.

Joy is the light, and the light is joy. You cannot access joy if you are emotionally blocked - if you are eating away at the communication lines between you and your creator. I've mentioned this before, but one of the reasons again that I did not leave my relationship earlier was because I kept thinking that if the light in me could just focus on the light in him, then all will be alright. No. My kryptonite was killing the light in me. I was eating my way to an early grave because I was not taking care of my body and my emotional health. I was letting other people's perceptions of me keep me in an unhealthy state. I was letting the fear of rejection and abandonment overrule my spiritual instincts, which were trying to tell me that joy was waiting for me on the other side of my kryptonite.

    My dear sister (and brother), it is time to reclaim your joy. Fear is an illusion. Its job is to tell your brain that you cannot make it on your own. Its job is to keep you alone and in the dark. Its mission is to keep you tethered to pain because that is where it is comfortable. It's safe to live in fear because you do not have to be responsible for your actions. You do not have to be accountable. You do not have to grow.

    But I am here to tell you that that is a lie. If you want joy, it requires you to seek the light. It demands that you be responsible for and accountable to your emotions. It requires self-reflection and awareness. It requires boldness. It requires a return to love. To love yourself is the greatest chain breaker - the greatest light.

In November 2017, I sought the light, and that required that I let go of the boundaries I had placed on the Divine and myself about what my exit should look like. I had to confront my grief, let it go and then forgive myself for holding onto it for so long. I had to return to joy, and so do you.

Post from 11/2/2018

One day, I decided that I love color...

♡ #fearlessfriday

#ILoveMeMore

Homework

What are three things, places or people that/who bring you joy? How can you incorporate those things into your daily living?

Chapter 7 ~ Kryptonite Killed Superwoman

"I can be changed by what happens to me. I refuse to be reduced by it" (Maya Angelou).

So, what is your kryptonite? What is the thing or person that distracts you from YOU? As I mentioned earlier, I came up with this concept when I found myself 50 pounds overweight from the stress of trying to run a profitable company of my own creation (*Average Girl Magazine*) and keep my then-husband happy. It didn't work. I was physically, financially and emotionally spent. My kryptonite was in trying to please everyone accept for myself. It was in trying to please everyone's expectation about what I should be.

Superwoman Syndrome
- Church/Community
- Fear of failure/success
- Family/kids
- Work
- Food/Drink
- Sex
- Shopping/Money

This is where we as women (and even men) lose ourselves. We try to please everyone with everything. We push aside our needs and dreams to make everyone else happy because we do not want people to hate us or think that we are selfish. That word, selfish, has been thrown at me for years. Every time I tried to put up a play or make a film, or even go out of town to speak at a conference, I was called "selfish." How many times has that word been thrown at you when you tried to do something for you?

As I mentioned in the previous chapter, the number one killer of women is heart attack followed by heart disease. That should really not be a surprise because women operate on a deeply primal and intuitive level from the heart. Again, the number one killer for us, women, is the very thing that drives us: the heart. Let's stop and analyze this more closely.

Women & Stress: The Consequences

#1 killer of women is Myocardial Infarction (heart attack) Followed by:

- Cardiovascular Disease (heart disease)
- Hypertension (high blood pressure)
- Obesity
- Cancer (breast & ovarian)

Intrapersonal Communication

Intrapersonal communication is defined as the ability to understand and appreciate one's innermost feelings. So, as I discussed earlier with Geneen Roth's book, *Women, Food & God*, one must have the ability to know what they are feeling and why. Again, why am I eating this whole carton of ice cream? Because I really want it? Or because I am upset, and I do not know how to or want to confront my innermost feelings for what I am upset about?

Interpersonal Communication

Interpersonal communication is the ability to understand and relate to others. In short, you have the ability to empathize or have compassion for people because you are able to put yourself in their shoes. Or, on a much deeper level, you may not have personally experienced x, y, z, but you recognize that another human being needs support and understanding at the moment. For example, I may not have born a still-born child, but as a mother, as a human being, I understand the depths of grief. I suffered at miscarriage at 10 weeks in 2003. I know grief well.

Before you can help others, you must first help yourself. But how do you do that when you are running on empty? I had to learn this the hard way. In June of 2015, I went to NY for a Black Theatre Conference and to see one of my short plays performed in a festival. I had this horrible cough which I attributed to my spring asthma/allergies. As I exited the subway near 42nd Street, the climb up the stairs nearly took my breath away. I puffed on my inhaler but received minimal relief. Something was definitely wrong. When I returned home, I put off going to see the doctor because I thought I just needed to keep taking my inhaler. A few days later, I found myself nearly unable to breathe. I went to the ER and sure enough, it was NOT my asthma. It was my thyroid. My T3 level was 434. The normal range is 71-171. The ER doctor looked at me sideways and said, "How are you still walking around?" In short, I should have been dead.

I was sent to an endocrinologist who diagnosed me with Hyperthyroidism, meaning, my thyroid was producing an exorbitant amount of thyroid into my circulatory and respiratory systems. Ironically, my little sister had been diagnosed with the same disease a few months earlier, but her condition was not as dire as mine, although we were both also diagnosed with the correlating disease, Grave's Disease, which is an enlarged goiter. I learned that this disease was not only hereditary but could be brought on by stress. Was I under a lot of negative stress? Absolutely! Another sign that my body was in trouble? I had lost 20 pounds in two weeks. Not normal at all.

My endocrinologist told me that less than 1% of persons with this disease go into remission and that I would probably have to be on medication all my life if I did well on it. The other alternative was to have the thyroid removed should the medication not work. I was devastated. How could this be happening to me? Easy! Not only was I stressed, but I was taking a low hormone birth control called Loestrine and I had given birth just six years prior to being diagnosed. Why am I telling you this? Because these are all the triggers for thyroid disease. But my high stressed life put me over the edge, so to speak.

If gone untreated, hyperthyroidism can cause the heart to stop working (aka, heart attack). It can also cause respiratory distress (you stop breathing). How many of us are walking around - no running ragged - not knowing that we are a ticking time bomb waiting to explode? I had to let some things go. My life depended on it.

One of the things I let go was other people's expectations of me. The stress of trying to please everyone, but especially my spouse, was too much. I also began to walk at least three times a week and I added drinking more water to my diet along with 3-5 servings of fruits and vegetables.

Two years later, I was in remission and off the medication. I was that 1% whose thyroid responded to medication, and then I went off the wagon. By 2016-2017, I was working double shifts, pushed by the pressure at home to "do my part." My kryptonite had returned with a vengeance. But I was not willing to let it take me down again. I'd officially had enough.

Remember in the previous chapter when I shared that when one is really ready to let go, they'll not put boundaries around the escape? Marianne Williamson said in her book, *The Law of Divine Compensation*, that "God is not bound by form." In prayer and meditation, I asked for a release from both the job and the marriage. I didn't put any parameters on what I needed to have happen before I gave up both. I simply asked God to release me: "Put where you need me to be," is what I said. And so, in November and December 2017, I released myself from my marriage and the double shifts.

Please know that I was terrified. I now had no job and no husband, but I was free and ready. I had removed the kryptonite from my life, and it was affirmed for me in these actions that I was not, nor do I ever want to be Superwoman. It costs too much.

In recognizing the source of anguish and turmoil I felt in my life, I was able to tap into my intrapersonal needs and create a new life - a new way - of communicating with myself. I now knew what my triggers were and how to deal with them appropriately. Instead of eating a gallon of ice cream, I now sat down with myself and asked, "What emotion am I trying to run away from or am not wanting to feel?" When I discovered what it was, I allowed myself to "sit" in it for a while (like 5 minutes to a half hour) and then I let it go.

And how did I do this? By repeating positive affirmations to myself. By understanding that this issue is only for the moment. That I am, at the core of my being, a good person who is worthy of forgiving herself so that she can love herself. But the biggest change in thought was this: I do not have the power to change the events that are happening at this moment. The only thing I have control over at any given moment is myself and my response/reaction to the issue.

In other words, I owned my role in my response to whatever the issue was at the moment. It is only when we can learn to do this that we are able and capable of tapping into interpersonal communication to then help others. Your family is no good if you are broken. When mom is broken, so is the family and the community.

Accessing Personal Awareness

So, what are other things we can do to help us break free from the life-damaging effects of our kryptonite? Here are a few strategies you can start today that will help you begin to tap into your intrapersonal intelligence. We must release the stress in order to begin our journey to authentic healing and purpose.

- Create a sacred, quiet space (the closet) – silence is golden
- Breathing – deep breathing; listen to the sound of your heart beating
- Yoga – stretching of the muscles, deep breathing and core strength/balance
- Journaling - writing is a form of therapy - scripture says, "Write it. Make it plain" (Habakkuk 2:2).

Meditation is by far one of the most effective strategies I want to encourage you to try - still the mind. "Meditation develops the capacity to question your mind. Without it, you are at the mercy of every thought, every desire, every wave of emotion" (Roth). There are many apps for meditation that you can download to your phone or Ipad/tablet. And please note that meditation is not for weird people nor is it complicated to do. You can start with two minutes or five and work your way up. Do it first thing in the morning when you arise (or after getting the kids off to school, which is what I do) because it stops the rambling of the mind. Again, prayer is you speaking to the Divine. Meditation is you listening to the Divine.

Let's be clear. You were made for more than whatever your "this" might be. You were not made to be anybody's whipping board or to carry someone else's pain. There is more to your life than "this." You are reading this book because something deep down inside of you is telling you - no, shouting - "I am more than *just*" Rebekah, Susan, Ann, or whatever your name may be. That voice you are hearing is YOU - the REAL you. It is your soul, and it's saying, "I am Worthy!"

Post from 12/19/18

How do you design a life you love? I started by first acknowledging that I was worthy of love, and that love had to come from deep within me, directed at me. Then, I had to sit down with me and forgive myself for everything I ever said or felt about myself that came from a place of fear and self-loathing. I was abandoned, but that did not diminish my worth. I was rejected, but that did not diminish my worth. I was beat down, but that did not diminish my worth. In short, to design the life you love, you begin by laying down the first to bricks: self-love and worthiness. "A wise woman builds her home, but a foolish woman tears it down with her own hands" (Proverbs 14:1, NLT). #wellnesswednesday #ILoveMeMore

Homework

What are three things that you love about the most confident woman in your life? What are three things you love about yourself? Create a vision board for the three things you love about yourself and put it somewhere where you will see it first thing in the morning and the last thing at night without effort.

Chapter 8 ~ Darling, It's Time to Jump!

"Too many of us our not living our dreams because we are living our fears" (Les Brown).

"What scares many of us about "jumping" is the fact that many of us have never seen anyone in our close circles do it or who has done it successfully (in our opinion, that's another conversation for later). We are terrified to create that business idea or pursue that degree because we do not have the template to follow. Guess what? You ARE the template! Do not wait for others to create the way for you. Stop chasing other people's dreams because you're afraid of what people would say if they knew what you really wanted to do. There's no one else in the world like you. You are the original and that means your dreams are too. Still afraid to "jump"? Then create a new circle and fill it with jumpers. I'd be happy to be your first."

So, what does it mean "to jump"? I heard Steve Harvey use this term several years ago, and at first, I wasn't quite sure how it applied to me, which is kind of sad considering that my entire life has been driven by the act of jumping: going to college, joining the military, starting a business, etc. So why wasn't I getting it when Steve said it? It was because I not only wasn't ready for the message, but also because I was looking at me (who I was or was not) in the wrong way. Case in point. Here's my post from December 11, 2018.

"Cinderella was a Jumper"

"We all know her story: the people closest to her felt that Cinderella was not good enough to be seen, let alone go to the royal ball and possibly attract the attention of a prince. We know what happens next: she gets the man and her "haters" are silenced forever. The end? No. Not hardly. In fact, that's not even the moral of this fairytale as many of us have been taught to believe.

Cinderella is not about getting a man - literally. It is about using what you have to achieve a goal. It's about determined faith in oneself and the job of the universe to give us our greatest good when we operate from the position of said faith. In short, Cinderella knew her worth. She refused to let others tell her what and who she was. Her clothes and an empty coffer did not define her. So, she called on faith (Fairy Godmother) who then gave her eyes to see that everything she needed to "become" was right there in front of her.

Cinderella did not leave her shoe on the palace steps on purpose. It wasn't an "accident" or a "coincidence" that it fell off. The universe is not arbitrary. It is purposeful, meaning your destiny will always find you because your dreams don't come to you; you come from it. It came with you. Like Cinderella, then, we must 1) know our worth, 2) lean on our faith, 3) open our eyes to what is in front of us and 4) take action - JUMP! Let today be the day that you become a JUMPER!"

Spread Your Wings and Fly

When I made the final decision to leave, I was TERRIFIED. I was going to have to go back home to my mother's house, but with two children this time. I had not prepared myself as well as she had wanted me and my sister to do; I had an education, but I was drowning in the spirit of lack and fear. The story of *Cinderella* has been told and taught to us incorrectly. It was never about getting a man; it was about knowing who and *whose* you are, owning your gifts and living life full out, in color and on purpose. The world has not the right to define you; You do! It's time to JUMP and see how high your wings can take you.

Post from 12/12/2018

What scares many of us about "jumping" is that many of us have never seen anyone in our close circles do it or knows of anyone who has done it successfully (in our opinion - that's another conversation for later). We are terrified to create that business idea or pursue that degree because we do not have a template to follow. Guess what? You ARE the template! Do not wait for others to create the way for you. Stop chasing other people's dreams because you're afraid of what people would say if they knew what you really wanted to do. There's no one else in the world like you. You are the original and that means your dreams are too. Still afraid to "jump"? Then create a new circle and fill it with jumpers. I'd be happy to be your first. 😁 ♡ #wellnesswednesday #ILoveMeMore #imjumping

Homework

JUMP! JUMP! JUMP! Start that business, go back to school, write that book! You only have one life to live. Why not love on it?!

Chapter 10 ~ There was Once a Woman Named Esther

> *"And he brought up Hadassah, that is, Esther, his uncle's daughter: for she had neither father nor mother, and the maid was fair and beautiful; whom Mordecai, when her father and mother were dead, took for his own daughter" (KJV 2:5-7).*

In the Hebrew bible, there is a chapter called the Book of Esther. Esther was a young Jewish girl who was taken from her family along with many other young girls from various parts of the country and eventually is chosen as the queen for Persian king, Ahasuerus. Ester spend years being groomed to be the pleasure of the king, but she had a secret. Esther was a Jew, a despised race that the king's cousin set out to have murdered.

When Ester's cousin, Mordecai, learned of the plan, he immediately went to Esther and told her that she must go to the king and ask him to spare her people. Well, Esther was terrified because no one could go to the king without being called for. The penalty for such a brazen act was death. Ester though long and hard about her cousin's request and the punishment for not only revealing what she was, but what she wanted.

After careful thought, meditation, prayer and fasting, Esther went to King Ahasuerus and made her request. Mordecai told her that her life and all that had happened to her before and upon entering the kingdom, had prepared her for this moment:

> "For if you keep silent at this time, relief and deliverance will rise for the Jews from another place, but you and your father's house will perish. And who knows whether you have not come to the kingdom for such a time as this?" (Ester 4:14, ESV).

And because of her strength and faith that she was made for a time such as this, the King granted her request. Esther risked her own personal safety to save her people because she realized that it was not just about her. The good and bad experiences she had experienced before becoming Queen, shaped and prepared her for this moment.

When I first contemplated telling my story publicly, I was so afraid of what people would say. I was afraid of a social death. But like Ester, I soon had to come to terms with the fact that I had to tell my story. I had to free myself and thus, help others to do the same. We are in the season of Esther. Each of you reading this book has a story of overcoming. Each of you has a gift that can change lives. And you are afraid to tell/share it because, like Ester, you know the risks. They are great and terrifying. But they are also not real.

In other words, fear is what has kept you immobile. Fear is what has brought you to the edge of the cliff. Fear tells you that you are not worthy of love. You are not worthy of healing. No one will believe you. No one will listen to you. This is fear's job. Its SOLE and ONLY purpose, as I've mentioned before, is to keep you from YOU. Many of you won't leave your toxic relationship because you think you can't make it. Fear has placed that tape recording in your head, and so EVERYTIME you get ready to leave, it starts blasting over the speakers so loud you cannot even see straight.

Esther must have looked out over the horizon and thought the same thing, but as with her, you were made for such a time as this. You MUST rise up and go to the king. You MUST reveal the truth of who you and *whose* you are. One of the things I mentioned earlier was that my mother did not seek counseling for us because she did not know about it, and probably could not have afforded it anyway. We are blessed to live in a day and time when counseling is available to us for

FREE. The YWCA is one of the greatest resources available to women suffering from all forms of abuse (National Domestic Violence Hotline, 1-800-799-7233).

    Scripture says: "Where no counsel is, the people fail: but in the multitude of counselors there is safety" (Proverbs 11:14, KJV). I sought counsel for myself with the YWCA when I left my marriage. I put my children in counseling too because the greatest gift I could ever give to them is sound mental health. And it was the greatest gift that I could give to myself because here I now stand. It was *never* just about me. And it is *not* just about you. Rise up, Esther! Your people need you.

Epilogue

A Road Map

How can you live your life full out, in color and on purpose? How can you work with the cards you've been dealt? Create a mission statement. Everyone should have a mission statement for their life. A road map, you can say. Here's mine:

Life/Artist Mission Statement
The mission of Rebekah Lynn Pierce is to be a positive inspiration to her fellow man/womankind through the light and joy of her spirit which resonates through her literary works thereby allowing her to be able to walk through opened doors of opportunity.

I encourage you to take some time and take inventory of who you are and what you feel you were meant to be or do. A mission statement does not have to be perfect, but it should reflect how you feel about yourself and your intentions for living the best life possible. Once you think you have the right words, design a beautiful frame for it and just like with the three things you love about yourself, put your mission statement in your sight. You can even put it on your social media pages, in your wallet/purse or as the wallpaper on your phone.

I also want to encourage you to fill a journal with daily affirmation statements. Here are a few that I recite every day, oftentimes more than once because … Lawd! ☺

*I am a problem solving, life empowering, soul connecting Divine spark of God.
*I was made in Love to Love.
*I am well able to provide for my family and home.
*I am relinquishing all anger, fear and pain. I am living my life full out and in color.
*I am traveling the world speaking life into women and girls empowering them to reclaim their authentic voices and power.
*All is well.

Remember, you were given this one life. Fill it with light, love and joy!

Rebekah

Rebekah L. Pierce – Mini Bio

Rebekah Pierce has been writing and teaching English literature for over 20 years. She is a lover of mystery novels that feature protagonists who have their own demons to fight as they save the day, so to speak. Her first novel, ***Murder on Second Street: The Jackson Ward Murders,*** is a blend of history and fiction. The plot is set during a very pivotal time in American history: 30 days before the infamous Black Tuesday, October 29, 1929 in the historic Negro neighborhood of Jackson Ward in Richmond, Virginia. In December 2014, Pierce released a new historical fiction novel also set in Richmond in 1862 called ***The Secret Life of Lucy Bosman***. The novel tells the story of a former slave mulatto named Lucy Bosman who risks her life to claim her inheritance at the height of the Civil War.

Over the years, Rebekah has also written and directed several award winning full-length and short plays several of which have been performed on Off-Broadway. In 2015, she released her first docu-short film based off of ***Murder on Second Street*** entitled, ***Black Wall Street: The Money, The Music & The People*** (www.blackwallstreetthemove.yolasite.com). The film blends documentary-style narrative featuring historic places and sites in Jackson Ward with the fictive thriller storyline of the novel. Pierce is currently writing a TV drama series based on the life of an African American female soldier returning home from Afghanistan called "**The War at Home.**"

    A veteran of the armed forces, Pierce is a member of several local writers' groups for both fiction and drama where her work has been widely received and supported. She resides in North Chesterfield, VA with her two children and mother.

Social Media

Facebook – www.facebook.com/rebekah.l.pierce
Instagram - @editor25
Twitter - @rebekahpierce
YouTube Channel – RLP Productions
& Rebekah Pierce

RESOURCES

All images used in this book were taken from my daily posts on my Facebook and Instagram pages. I do not own the images presented in this book; their sources are listed in the images or are referenced as "unknown." All books referenced in this work are available on Amazon.com:

- Blume, Judy. *Are you there God? It's me, Margaret!*
- Pierce, Rebekah L. *Kryptonite Killed Superwoman.*
- Roth, Geneen. *Women, Food and God.*
- Williamson, Marianne. *The Laws of Divine Compensation.*

Made in the USA
Middletown, DE
08 June 2019